MW01488208

EYES AND NO EYES

BOOK 2: BY POND AND RIVER

Be sure to look for the rest of the Eyes and No Eyes series, as well as many other great books to supplement your nature study at-
www.livingbookpress.com

This edition published 2021
by Living Book Press
Copyright © Living Book Press, 2021

First published in 1903.

ISBN: 978-1-922619-89-1 (softcover)
            978-1-922619-90-7 (hardcover)

All rights reserved. No part of this publication may be reproduced, stored in a retrieval system, or transmitted in any other form or means – electronic, mechanical, photocopying, recording or otherwise, without the prior permission of the copyright owner and the publisher or as provided by Australian law.

A catalogue record for this book is available from the National Library of Australia

Eyes and No Eyes
Book 2

BY POND AND RIVER

BY

Arabella B. Buckley
(Mrs. Fisher)

PUBLISHER'S NOTE

We at Living Book Press are extremely proud to bring you this release of Eyes and No Eyes, originally published by Cassell.

Some of the old images were not of a high enough quality to reprint so we have included some of the black and white images from the original as well as many high quality photographs to accompany the text throughout.

Because this book represents a broad overview of the nature we will find around us the images may sometimes be of similar creatures and plants that are native to other regions than the United Kingdom where the story was first set. This is to help children appreciate that many animal and plant families share similar traits and can be found in many parts of the world, some may even be in their own backyard, as well as provide an opportunity for those who can't access the great outdoors to see nature up close.

We hope these new editions bring a lot of joy to your homes, and that they will help children everywhere take a deeper look at the natural world surrounding them.

Living Book Press.
2021.

CONTENTS

PREFACE.

These books are intended to interest children in country life. They are written in the simplest language, so as to be fit for each class to read aloud. But the information given in them requires explanation and illustration by the teacher. I have, in fact, tried to make each lesson the groundwork for oral teaching, in the course of which the children should be encouraged to observe, to bring in specimens, and to ask questions. Then when the chapter is read and re-read, as is the case with most school books, it will become part of the child's own knowledge.

No one can be more aware than I am how very slight these outlines arc, and how much more might have been given if space permitted. But I hope that much is *suggested*, and a teacher who loves nature will fill in the gaps.

The charming illustrations will enable the children to identify the animals and plants mentioned.

ARABELLA B. BUCKLEY
(Mrs. Fisher).

LESSON I.
A FROG'S LIFE.

CROAK, croak, croak, we hear the frogs in the month of March. They make a great deal of noise in this month, because they are just awake from their winter's sleep, at the bottom of the pond.

The mother frogs are laying their tiny dark eggs in the water. Each egg is not bigger than a grain of sand. But it has a coat of jelly, and this jelly swells and swells in the water, till it is as large as a pea, with a little black dot in the middle. The jelly lumps all cling together. You may see them in almost any pond, driven up to the side by the wind.

Soon the dark speck lengthens. A head grows at one end, and a tail at the other. The head has a mouth, but no eyes as yet. The tail has a fin all round it, and the tadpole wriggles about in its slimy bed.

In about a week it wriggles out of the jelly, and hangs by its mouth to the weeds. Then two curious tufts grow on each side of its head. It uses these tufts to breathe, by taking air out of the water. You can see them if you dip a glass into the pond and catch a few tadpoles.

By this time the tadpole has let go of the weed and is swimming about. A sharp beak has grown on to his mouth. He uses it to tear off pieces of weed to eat. Now he grows eyes, nose-holes and flat ears. His tufts shrivel up, and a cover grows over them, so that you cannot see them. They are now like the gills of a fish. He gulps water in at his mouth and sends it out through the cover. As it passes, the gills take the air out of it, and so the tadpole breathes.

Soon two small lumps appear on each side of his body, behind the cover, just where it joins his tail. They grow larger and larger, till at last two hind legs come out. These legs grow very long and strong, and he uses them to swim. Two front legs are growing as well, but you cannot see them, because they are under the cover. In a few days these peep out, but they are short and stumpy.

Our tadpole has now four legs and a tail. He has four toes on the front feet, and five toes on the hind feet, with a skin between the toes. So his hind legs are web-footed, and this helps him to swim.

He comes to the top of the water much more often than before, and sends a bubble of air out of his mouth. What do you think has happened? The gills under his cover have closed up, and a small air-bag has grown inside him. So he comes up to breathe in the air through his mouth, instead of taking it out of the water through his gills.

Now he likes to jump on a piece of weed and sit in the shade. He does not want his tail any longer, for he can swim quite well with his legs. So his tail is slowly sucked in to feed his body.

There you have your little frog. If you look through the web of his foot at the sun, you will see that he has

red blood now. But it is not warm blood like ours. He is always cold and clammy, because his blood moves slowly.

He has a number of teeth in the top of his mouth, and such a curious tongue. It is tied down to the front of his mouth, and the tip, which is very sticky, lies back down his throat. He does not eat weed now. He feeds on insects and slugs. He catches them by throwing out his tongue and drawing it back very quickly.

He lives chiefly on land during the summer if he is not eaten by ducks, rats, or snakes. Then he drops to the bottom of the pond to sleep in the mud all the winter.

LIFE CYCLE OF A FROG.

LESSON II.

THE DRAGON-FLY AND HIS COMPANIONS.

Every country boy or girl, who wants to learn about water animals, should make a pond net. You have only to get a willow twig, and bind it into a hoop with string. Then make a muslin bag and sew a small stone in the bottom of it, and sew the mouth of the bag on to the hoop. Get a stick out of the hedge and fasten to it a long piece of string. Split the string near the end, and tie it to the two sides of the hoop. Then you have a net which you can let down and fish up animals from the bottom of the pond. You had better have a wide-mouthed bottle as well in which you can put what you catch. I know a shady pond just outside a farmyard at the turn of a lane. There on a bright sunny day the insects are often very busy.

MAYFLY

In one corner of the pond the little whirligig beetles are swimming round and round, making circles in the water. Their shining black backs look almost green in the sun. Every now and then one jumps up to catch a fly in the air, or another dives down to eat a grub. Drop your net into the water and bring it up quickly under a beetle, and put him in the bottle so that you can see him. You will think that he has four eyes, for each of his two eyes is divided. One half looks up into the air, and one half looks down into the water. So as he whirls about, he can see the flies in the air and the grubs in the water.

Gnats are flitting to and fro over the pond, and there is quite a crowd of those large flies with gauze wings which we call May-flies. And now a more splendid fly, three inches long, with four big gauze wings rises out of the bulrushes and flies over the pond.

All boys know the dragon-fly. His lovely wings are covered with cross-bars filled with air, and they glitter in the sunshine with red, blue, and green colours. He has a long tail and a thick body with six legs, and a round head with huge eyes.

Each eye has more than ten thousand tiny windows in it, so that he can see up and down, right and left, as he darts

DRAGON-FLY EYES

about, killing the butterflies and moths that come in his way. Then he settles down on a plant or bush by the water-side, and rests till he starts off again across the pond.

If you go often in April to a pond where dragon-flies are, you may perhaps see one begin its life in the air. This is how it happens.

Under the water a large insect crawls up the stem of a plant. He has a body as big as a dragon-fly and has six legs. But he has a curious dull look in his face, and where his wings should be there are only two short stumps.

DRAGON-FLY LARVA EATING A FISH

A DRAGON-FLY EMERGES.

He crawls very slowly up the stem, till he comes out of the water into the air. Then a strange thing happens. The skin of his back cracks, and out creeps a real dragon-fly.

First his head, then his body with its six legs and four soft, crumpled wings, and lastly his tail. He cannot fly yet. He stands by his old empty skin, and slowly stretches out his wings to the sun. In a few hours they are long and strong and hard. Then he is ready to fly over the pond and feed.

This is how the dragon-fly comes up to the air. You will not find him so easily under the water, but we will try next week with our net. We have seen so much at the top of the pond to-day that we have not had time to dredge in the mud below.

LESSON III.

DOWN BELOW.

To-day we will use our net. Hold the stick tight, and throw the net out into the pond as a fisherman throws a fly. Then the stone will sink the net slowly. If now you pull it gently through the mud and water-plants, you are sure to get something.

Bring the net to land and lower it on the grass, and put all you can find into the clear water in the bottle. You may find a little fish, or some tadpoles, or water-snails. Or there may be one of the curious creatures shown at

DRAGON-FLY NYMPH

the top of this page. I am sure you would not think this
was the grub of a dragon-fly. But it is. It is a long insect,
all joints, with six legs, and eyes something like those of
the dragon-fly. It has no wings, but a curious kind of arm,
with pincers at the end, comes out from under its chin.

This is really part of its under-lip. It is called a mask,
and has a hinge, so that it can be folded back under the
chin. Now when the grub wants food, he waits quietly in
the mud, till a beetle or a water-bug passes by. Then he
throws out his mask, and catches his prey with the pincers.

Look next at the end of its tail. Sometimes it is pointed,
sometimes it opens; out like the leaves of a flower. When
it is open the grub draws water in, and uses the air in it
to breathe.

Then it shoots the water out and so pushes itself across
the pond.

This dragon-fly grub lives at the bottom of the pond for two years. So you ought to catch one some time if you try. It changes its skin many times, and grows some wing-stumps. Then it creeps up a stem, as we saw in the last lesson, and becomes a dragon-fly.

And now what is this in our net? At first you may think it is only a bit of stick, or a piece of mud with little stones in it, or a number of bits of grass matted together. And so it is. But there is something alive inside. If you look carefully you can see the head of an insect sticking out with six legs behind it. This is a soft little creature called a caddis-worm. If you clear off the pieces of grass, or stick, or small stones, or shells, you will find the soft grub inside. It has six legs and a number of little tufts

CADDIS-WORM

CADDIS FLY (ABOVE) AND LARVA (OPPOSITE)

under its body. It breathes with these tufts just as the tadpole does with its tufts.

You may often see caddis-worms creeping along the bottom of brooks, looking like tiny, moving bundles of sticks or stones. You may pick them up without using a net. They build these cases round themselves to try to protect their soft bodies, which the fish like to eat.

CADDIS-GRUBS AND CADDIS-FLY.

By-and-by they will turn into little yellow-brown flies like moths. They rise and fall in the air over the water in the evening. We did not see them with the May-flies and gnats, because they do not like the sunshine.

You will very likely fish out a good many little water grubs in your net. But you must look carefully, for they are very small. Some have tufts all along their sides. These are the grubs of the gnats and May-flies you saw flying over the pond. They all live some time in the water. And when they come out into the air they do not live more than a few hours.

MAY-FLY ON THE WATER

STICKLEBACK

LESSON IV.

THE STICKLEBACK'S NEST.

It was a lovely day in May. The sun was shining, the grass was green, and the bushes on the banks of the river Thames were covered with fresh leaves.

In a hollow place in the river a little fish was building a nest. The fish was a stickleback. It was not more than two inches long. It had three spines sticking up on its back. Boys often catch this fish, and keep it in bottles or sell it to people who have aquariums.

It was more pleasant to watch him at work under the shade of the bushes. He brought little pieces of fine root-threads and narrow grass, and made them into a tiny saucer at the bottom of the river. Then he brought more pieces and stuck them on with slime from his mouth. In this way he made sides and a round roof. When he had done, the nest was as big as a large gooseberry.

It was about six inches below the top of the water, and

had a hole right through it. When the stickleback put his head out at one end, his tail stuck out at the other. But he had not built it to live in. He wanted it for the eggs of his young ones.

He was a lovely little fish with a shining back, and bright red belly. He had a bluish green eye that shone like a jewel.

Now that his nest was built he swam off to fetch a mate. He soon came back with another fish, not so bright as himself. He played with her, and drove her, and coaxed her, till at last she went in at one hole of the nest and, after a little while, came out at

STICKLEBACK PROTECTING HER TERRITORY

the other end.

She had deposited a tiny packet of yellow eggs, which she left behind her. Then she went away and took no more care of them.

The father stickleback now went through the nest and took charge of the eggs. Each egg was not bigger than a poppy seed, and the whole bunch was very tiny. He shook the nest up and poked the eggs into a snug, safe corner. Then he swam over the top of the nest, waving his fins, so that fresh water went in and out.

Sometimes he went into the nest and brought out some dirty sand in his mouth. This he puffed away into the water. You see he wanted to keep the nest clean.

He did this every day for three weeks, till the eggs were

19

hatched. Then a number of tiny fish came out. They were so small and transparent that you would think no other fish would see them. But the stickleback knew better. There were plenty of hungry fish watching to eat the tiny fry, which were very weak and had to carry a bag of food under their body, to suck in till they could eat.

So the brave little stickleback stuck up his three spines, and dashed angrily at any fish which snapped at his little ones. He seized their fins, and struck at their eyes and drove them away.

He made a small round place in the sand at the bottom of the river and gathered the little sticklebacks into it, and there he watched over them. Even after their spines were grown and they could swim boldly, he followed them out into the river to see that they were safe.

You may find plenty of stickleback's nests in rivers and ponds, if you look carefully for them. Or if you catch several sticklebacks in a bottle and put them in a large pan with plenty of weeds and food, most likely you will see a stickleback build his nest, and learn what a good father he is.

LESSON V.

THE KINGFISHER.

Hush! Do not make a noise! There is a kingfisher sitting on the bough of the willow tree hanging over the river. If we once startle him, he will fly away and we shall not see him again.

How lovely he looks against the grey leaves. With his long beak and his stumpy tail he is not much larger than a sparrow, yet he seems to wear all the colours of the rainbow.

He has a bright blue streak down his back, his head and wings are a lovely green, with blue spots on the tips of the feathers. His beak is black. His chin and throat are white. He has a red streak behind his eye, with soft white feathers beyond, and his breast is like shining cop-

KINGFISHER DIVING

per. Even his feet are red, and look quite gay against the dull branch.

He is peering down into the quiet pool under the willow, watching the fish swimming below. There! he has darted down to the water. Now he is up again with something in his mouth. It is a small minnow. He taps its head against the branch, and gulps it down, head first.

Once more, and still one more fish he catches in the same way. While he is eating the last, another kingfisher comes and perches by his side. This is his mate, who has been fishing a little way off. She is not quite so bright as he is, and has a little bit of red under her chin.

Now they are going home, and they fly away crying "Seep-seep-seep" as they go. They live in the trees and bushes by the side of the river. For you must always re-member that birds do not live in nests. The nest is only a cradle for their eggs and their little ones. As soon as they are able to fly, the young birds leave it with their parents,

EMERGING WITH A FISH

and do not often live in a nest again, till they make one for their own eggs.

I do not think you will easily find a kingfisher's nest, so I must tell you about it. When the mother wants to lay her eggs, the kingfishers dig a tunnel in the bank, and when it is made they dart into it so fast that you cannot see where they go.

But if you could know where it is and dig down from above, you would find a snug chamber which measures about six inches across. At the bottom of this chamber are a number of fish bones which the old birds have put there. They are mixed up together so that they make a nice open floor, where the wet can get away.

On the fish bones lie some shining white eggs. There will be seven, if the mother has laid as many as usual. And, if the eggs are hatched, there will be seven little birds. Each bird will have all the lovely colours of which I have told you. The only difference between them and the old birds is that their beaks are shorter.

Though you may, perhaps, not find a kingfisher's nest, you will very likely see some young birds on the river. I was once out with a friend who was fishing, and while his rod was over the water, all at once two small kingfishers flew up and settled upon it. They rested a moment, and then flew on. He had only just thrown his fly again on to the water, when two more kingfishers flew up and sat on the rod. They, too, soon went on. It was clear that they were young birds just out of the nest and could not fly far.

The kingfishers are the brightest birds you can see on the river. They look so pretty among the green leaves, and hovering over the water, that if you have once seen them, you will want to see them again.

KINGISHER RETURNING TO ITS NEST

WATER-VOLE

LESSON VI.
THE WATER-RAT, OR WATER-VOLE.

Have you ever seen a water-rat? I do not mean a land-rat swimming in the water, but a water-rat, or *water-vole*, as he ought to be called, for he is not a true rat. I saw one once when he did not see me. What do you think he was doing? He was sitting up on his hind legs, and in his front paws he held a piece of the leaf of the sweet yellow flag, which grows so thickly by the river. It was that part of the leaf near the root which is thick and juicy. He was

CAN YOU SEE THE ENTRANCE TO THE BURROW?

gnawing it so busily that he did not see me at first.

He was a stout little fellow, not quite so big as a rat. He feeds on plants. When he cannot get pieces of yellow flag he eats duckweed, or even the bark of young willows. I could see that he had a short, thick neck and round head, with a short snout. His eyes were small, and I could scarcely see his ears, they were so thickly covered with fur. His round tail was not very long and had short hairs on it.

I sat down very quietly on the bank, not far from him. And presently he looked round and saw me. But as I did not move perhaps he did not think I was alive, for he went on munching his leaf.

At last I touched a dead leaf with my foot. His ears heard quickly enough. He turned his little bright eyes to me, and in a second he was in the water and swam away.

I was too late to see him go into his hole, but I found one not far from the flags, just under the water.

I knew I should not find his home; for the water-voles make long burrows. I went for several days to the same place, and took some bread to leave there. At last one day, as I sat watching, out came my little friend and ate the bread. After that we met several times, and he became quite tame. But I had to be very careful. The least thing frightened him, and plop he went, into the water!

If you go often to a pond or river, when all is very quiet in the evening or early morning, you may sometimes see a water-vole swimming in the water, or feeding on the bank. He has beautiful yellow teeth. The lower ones are large and show very clearly above his short lower lip.

The young water-voles are such pretty little creatures. They are born in a nest of dry grass, which the old voles make in the burrow, and when they come out they swim

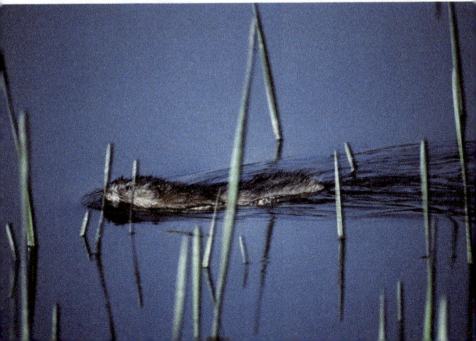

about with the old ones, and feed on the duckweed.

But though the water-vole lives mostly in the water, he can come on land to gather his winter store. He is often a great trouble to the farmer, for he likes the carrots and potatoes and even the broad beans, which grow in the fields, and he comes in the evening to eat them and to carry pieces back to his home.

A farmer once dug out a water-vole's burrow and found enough pieces of potato and mangoldwurzel to fill a gallon measure.

WATER-HEN

LESSON VII.
THE WATER-HEN AND THE COOT.

IF your way to school lies along a river-path, where trees hang over the water, you will very likely have seen a water-hen and her little ones. Perhaps you may know where a nest is, either among the rushes, or on a bough of a tree overhanging the water.

It is made of dead rushes, and though it is quite close to the water, it is dry and warm. If you are bathing you may look in. You will find about eight pale-grey eggs spotted with red-brown patches. Or perhaps some of the eggs may be hatched, and then the young birds will be hidden

BALD COOT AND YOUNG

with their mother in the rushes. They are little black balls of fluff with red on their heads and white tail-feathers, and they can run and swim directly they are born. All the time you are looking, the mother, hidden in the rushes, will cry *"Crr-ook, crr-ook"* to drive you away.

She is a black bird, about as big as a pigeon, with a bright red forehead and yellow beak. And she has white feathers on the edge of her wings and under her tail. When she is in the water, she keeps jerking her head down, so that you see the white feathers, and even her green legs with their red garters.

Very soon after the young water-hens are hatched, they slip out of the nest and swim round her. If you are lying very still among the bushes, you may perhaps see them all come out on to the bank, to feed on worms or snails. Then you can notice that their feet are not webbed like a duck's feet, but all four toes are separate.

But if you make the least noise, the mother will cry *"Krek-krek"* to her little ones, and they will dive into the water and swim to a safe place among the rushes. They will not go back to the nest, and even if you beat the rushes with a stick they will not move. They know that they are safer in their hiding place.

This bird is often called a moor-hen and she does go to the moors sometimes. But Water-hen is her better name.

And now, if there is a large lake anywhere near, you will see the water-hen there, and another bird, which you may think is the same, for she jerks her head and dives just in the same way. But if you look you will see that this second bird has not got a red forehead, but a large, bald patch on its head, and it is larger than the water-hen.

It is a bird called the coot, and often the "bald-headed coot," because of its bald patch. If you see one on the bank feeding on seeds or insects, you will notice that it has a wavy skin round each of its three front toes, though they are not joined together.

But the coot is not easy to see, for she is very shy. She runs up a tree, or dives under water, before you can get near her. She has sharp claws, which help her to climb, and which will hurt you if you catch her alive.

She builds her nest among the flags or rushes, almost touching the water. Sometimes her little ones are drowned when there is a flood.

If a boat comes near her nest, she slips off it into the rushes and cries *"Kew-kew"* to entice you away. If you find it, you will see about ten eggs in it. They are like the water-hen's eggs, but larger, and the spots are darker and smaller. If the eggs are hatched, you will know the little birds by their bald patch, though they are black, fluffy balls just like those of the water-hen.

You will not find the coot in rivers; nor will you find her on the ponds in the winter. Then she starts off with a number of other coots to the sea in the south of England, and stays till spring comes again.

SITTING ON ITS NEST.

WATER SCORPION

LESSON VIII.

THE WATER–BUGS.

WHEN you go home from school, if you pass a pond, you are almost sure to be able to find one, or more, of the three water-bugs of this lesson, and I want you to look at them.

The first is a long, thin, black insect. He walks on top of the water, looking like a needle on legs. He is sometimes called a "needle-bug," but more often a "water-measurer," because he seems to measure the water with his legs as he runs.

He has very fine hairs under his body and on his legs. The air between these hairs prevents him from getting wet and being drowned. He has two long feelers, and a long thin beak. His legs and body are a reddish colour and his wings a glossy black.

If you watch him, you will see him start all at once

across the pond. He is catching a water-fly. Then he will hold it in his front claws, and suck the juice out of its body. Though the water-measurer has wings, he does not often fly.

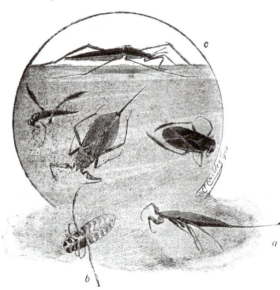

A. WATER-SCORPION. B. WATER-BOATMAN.
C. WATER-MEASURER

The next water-bug is not so thin. He is about an inch long, and has a flat body with grey wings folded across it. He has only very short feelers, and his front legs are thick and strong, with pincers at the end, and this is why he is called the "water-scorpion." He uses these pincers to seize the insects in the water, and sucks them dry through his sharp beak.

He swims under water very slowly, or crawls in the mud, and is easily caught. You may catch him too when he comes up to get air. This he does in a very funny way. He has two long bristles at the end of his tail. When he puts these together they make a tube like a hollow straw. He comes near the top of the water, and thrusts out the end of this tube into the air, and draws some into his body. The eggs of the mother water-scorpion are stuck on to the leaves of water-plants, and look like seeds.

The last water-bug I am sure you know.

He is a little fellow, rather like a beetle, with six legs, two of them being very long ones; and he swims upside down, rowing himself along with these two legs, as if they

WATER-BOATMAN

were oars. This is why he is called a "water-boatman."

He has a long, sucking beak, but you will hardly see it unless you dip him out with a glass and look close. For as he swims upside down, the bug bends his head down on his chest, so that his beak lies between his legs.

His eyes at the side of his head are very large, so that he can look both down and up. This is very useful, for he swims under tadpoles and grubs, and catches them in his claws. Then he bites them with his sharp beak, and sucks out their soft body. He is always swimming in the water, or crawling in the mud. In the evening he sometimes comes out and flies to another pond or ditch.

The mother water-boatman lays small, long, white eggs on stems and leaves in the water. You may often find them in March, and in April you may see the little bugs swimming upside down like their parents.

WATER-MEASURER

If you take the trouble, you may catch these three water-bugs in a net, and put them in a glass, and see all I have told you.

WATER SCORPION

BULL-HEAD

LESSON IX.
ALONG THE RIVER.

LET us stroll a short distance along the river. How pretty it is, with the evening sun shining through the trees! What a number of little creatures are enjoying themselves in the air and in the water!

Pale little Tommy, who has come from London for a holiday, slips his hand in mine and says, "I wish I could live in the country." When he goes back to his own home in a narrow street, where there is only a hard pavement instead of green grass, and no shady trees nor flowing water, he will remember this walk by the river.

Look at those fish, about three inches long, swimming up and down under the bridge. Those are bull-heads. They are called so because they have such broad, thick heads. And they have a sharp spine on each side of their head, which we might call the bull's horns. You will feel those spines if you try to hold them in your hand. The kingfisher knows them well enough, if he tries to swallow one, for they stick in his throat.

You boys call them "millers' thumbs." I wonder why you think that millers have broad thumbs? The bull-heads hide under stones, and eat water insects, and the eggs of other fish. Ah! Fred has caught one and put it in the bottle. Now Tommy can see what a lovely eye the bull-head has, and the red, green, brown and yellow colours on his scales.

KINGFISHER EATING A BULL-HEAD

How busy those flies are with long wings and three long bristles on their tails. They are Mayflies rising and falling over the water. They are not feeding, for May-flies do not eat, and

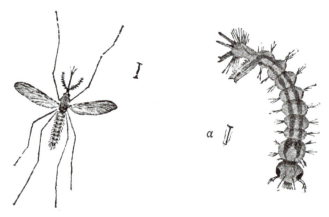

GNAT AND GNAT GRUB.

only live a few hours. But they have lived a long time under water as grubs, like the dragon-fly grub. They only want now to lay their eggs and die.

The gnats flying over that quiet pool near the mill are quite different. One has just pricked my hand and sucked some blood, so I know that he can feed. But then gnats have not had so long a life in the water as the May-flies.

Those gnats flying over the pool were only born a few

GNAT LARVAE AND PUPA.

weeks ago. Their mother laid some sticky eggs, each not bigger than the point of a pin, and left them in a packet on the top of the still water. They were very soon hatched, and a number of grubs came out, looking like very tiny worms with fine hairs on their sides. Each swam about in the water and ate specks of weed.

Why do you think they swam with their heads down? Because they could only breathe near their tails, and so had to stick them up in the air.

In about three weeks each grub had changed his skin three times. The fourth time he came out with a wrapper round him, and if you could have looked at him then, you would have seen a perfect gnat, with wings, cuddled up inside.

Now he had to creep out, and that was very risky. For if he fell in the water he would be drowned. So he stretched himself very carefully on the top of the pool, and began to push his head through a slit in the wrapper.

Then he drew himself gently out, and stood on tiptoe on the empty skin, which floated like a boat on the water.

ALMOST READY TO HATCH

He spread his wings, and then he was safe and flew away. Sometimes the wind blows him over before he can get out, and then he is drowned.

If you take a pail of water out of a pond in May, and keep it in the open air, you may be able to see a gnat grow up, for there will most likely be a great many in it. But you must have sharp eyes, for they are very tiny.

And now the sun is setting and birds and beasts and flowers are all going to rest. Soon the night-moths and the owls and bats will be coming out. We must go home.

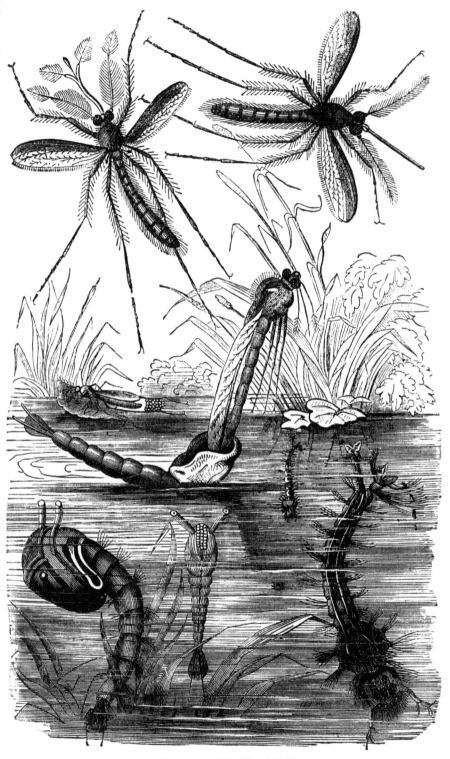

THE LIFECYCLE OF A GNAT

RIVER OTTER EATING FISH.

LESSON X.

THE OTTER FAMILY.

ABOUT five o'clock one fine morning in May, Tom, the gamekeeper's son, was examining the traps set for weasels, stoats, and other vermin. His way led him over a bridge across the river, and as he came near it he heard a strange whistling noise.

Now, Tom was a Devonshire lad, and all country boys in the West of England have sharp ears for the calls of animals. Tom knew that this cry came from a father or mother otter who were fishing in the river with their little ones.

Just below the bridge, where the bank was very high, there grew an old willow tree, with branches hanging over the river. The water had washed away the bank under the

MOTHER OTTER WITH CUBS

willow, so that there was a big hole between its strong roots.

Now, Tom knew that this hole was the home of some otters. Many a time the otter-hounds had stood in the water near this hole baying with all their might. But they could not get in, and the otters took care not to come out.

The hounds were far away now, and everything was very quiet in the early morning. So Tom lay down in the thick grass at the top of the bank and waited. By-and-bye on came the otters, swimming smoothly along with only their noses above water.

The old otters swam so quietly that Tom would not have known they were there. But the young otters were playing and twisting about, so that first their brown furry backs, and then their white bellies, shone in the light of the early morning sun, and the water splashed about them.

The river was very broad in this place, and just opposite

45

the willow was a small island. Tom was so well hidden
in the tall grass that the otters had no idea that he was
there. So one by one they scrambled up on the island,
each with a fish in its mouth. Then they each took hold
of their fish with their front feet, and began to eat just
behind the head. They ate on till they nearly reached the
tail and then left that.

While they were eating, Tom could see what they were
like. They had long bending bodies, and broad, flat heads,

and their mouths and noses were short and broad. Their feet were webbed like duck's feet, but each foot had very sharp claws at the end. Their fur was a lovely soft brown, but the long hairs on the old otters were coarse, and they did not look so soft as the little ones. Their tails were thick and strong, and very useful for helping them to swim.

The father tore the fish with his teeth quite fiercely, and sometimes threw small pieces to the young ones, who had soon finished their tiny fish. At last all was eaten up, except the heads and tails. Then the father otter slid down the bank, and the others followed him, and they all went to fish again.

There are fewer otters than there used to be in the rivers of England. But they are still to be found in many places. Only, if you want to see them at home, you must get up early in the morning.

LESSON XI.
FLOWERS FOR THE SHOW.

"WHERE are you going, Peggy?" asked Peter, as he passed her in the lane, one Saturday afternoon in July.

"I am going to look for flowers, for the flower-show next week. I shall not gather them, but I want to see what I can find."

"May I go with you? "

"Yes, if you can keep a secret. I want to make quite a new kind of nosegay, of flowers that grow in the water."

"But they will all fade if you put them in a bunch."

WHITE AND YELLOW WATER LILLIES

DUCKWEED

"I am not going to put them in a bunch. I am going to get one of father's large zinc pans which he uses for the dogs' food, and let the plants float in the water."

So Peggy and Peter started off to their favourite pond.

"See, Peter, I must have one of those lovely yellow 'water-lilies,' with its large, shiny green leaf, and one of its curious seed-boxes, which remain after the yellow flower-leaves have fallen off. I know that this plant has a thick stem in the mud at the bottom of the pond, and the long stalks grow right up, so that the leaves float on the top of the water. Little beetles crawl inside the flower and get honey from under the small yellow flower-leaves inside.

Then I must have some of those white stars with yellow in the middle. They look so pretty among their small green leaves, which are cut into three half-rounds. That is the 'water-crow-foot,' and if you hook a bit in with

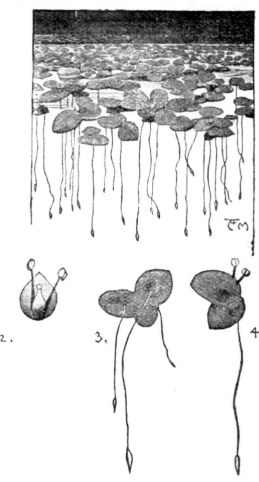

your stick we shall see that it has some other leaves under water, which are cut into strips like fine blades of grass."

"Why should it have two kinds of leaves, Peggy?"

"One set are its floating leaves to keep the flowers above water, where the insects can get at them, and the others are lighter and can spread out in the water without making so much green leaf. And look, Peter, the yellow lines on the white flowers point straight to the narrow

I. DUCKWEED. 2, 4. DUCKWEED FLOWERS.
3. ATTACHMENT OF THE ROOTS.

end of the flower-leaf, where the insects find the honey.

"Then I must have some duckweed. It will cover the pan so nicely."

"But the duckweed is not pretty, Peggy. It is all leaves."

"No, Peter, that is just what it is *not*. Paul told me the

WHITE BOGBEAN (OPPOSITE)

other day that the duckweed has no real leaves. Each plant is a little bit of stem with a thin root hanging down in the water. Very tiny flowers sometimes grow in a little split in the side of the stem. I shall try to get one of these, but they are so very small, and are only made of two little dust-bags and a seed-box. But the duckweed will float on the water.

"Now, Peter, I want to find a 'bog-bean' in flower. I am afraid it is rather late in the year, but there are some, I know, at the shallow end of the pond You must look for a large spike of pink-white flowers, shaped something like wide blue-bells and lined with a number of white hairs. Ah! here is one with the buds just opening; it will be all right for Wednesday.

"Now we must have one more. A little plant called the 'water-milfoil,' which is almost ill under water, except the spike of tiny pink flowers which stands straight up in the air. Look at its fine leaves arranged in stars round the stem. They lie out so well in the water. If you look very carefully at the flowers, you will see that the top ones have only dust-bags in them, and the lower ones only seed-boxes. But they are so small it is not easy to see this.

"Now I must not choose any more, for I must describe each one on my show-card, and it will take a long time."

WATER-MILFOIL

LESSON XII.

PEGGY'S WATERPLANTS.

WHEN Wednesday came, Peggy's pan was ready. She had taken it to the pond, and dipped it gently under the duckweed. She brought it up quite full, and picked it over very carefully, leaving only the best plants. Then she carried it to the show-room.

There she put the yellow lily into the middle of the pan, so that the flower, and the stalk with the seed-vessel, fitted into the hollow between the ears of the large green leaf just at the leafstalk. Next she put pieces of the water-crowfoot here and there, the pretty white blossoms streaked with

YELLOW WATER-LILY

yellow resting upon the top of the water.

She stuck two spikes of bog-bean, with their leaves, one on each side of the water-lily. Lastly, she put spikes of the water-milfoil round the edge of the pan. Their leaves made little green stars in the water all the way round, and their tiny pink flower-spikes made a lovely edge.

Then she wrote her card. This is what she said:

1. The yellow water-lily grows in the pond near the farm. It has a thick stem rooted in the mud down at the bottom. I saw it once when they cleaned the pond. We see nothing on the top of the water in March. But in May the large shining green leaves have grown to the top of the water on long stalks. They are shaped rather like a heart, but are pointed at the tip.

In June the buds come up. They are like green knobs tipped with yellow. But as they grow bigger, the five

54

outer leaves, or *sepals*, open, and they are quite yellow inside. Then we can see the small inner flower-leaves, or *petals*, arranged in two rows; after them come a number of stamens, made of thin threads, with dust-bags on the top. Then right in the middle is the seed-box, or *ovary*. It is shaped like a water-bottle with a round cushion on the top, and has a number of sticky points, which lie on the cushion in the shape of a star. Little beetles are often found in the flowers. They fly in, and suck the honey at the back of the petals.

2. The water-crowfoot grows in our pond. It is a kind of buttercup. It has five outer green leaves, or sepals. They turn back against the

WATER-BUTTERCUP, WITH ITS TWO KINDS OF LEAVES.

WATER-CROWFOOT

DUCKWEED

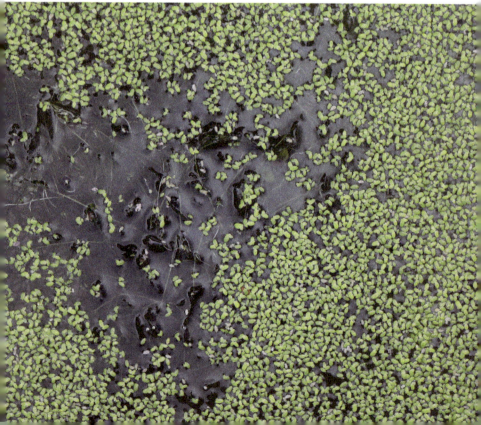

stem when the flower is open. They often fall off. There are five white petals. They are streaked with yellow near the middle of the flower, where there are drops of honey. After the petals, come many stamens, and then, in the middle of the flower, a number of seed-boxes, each with one seed inside.

The water-crowfoot has two kinds of leaves. The leaves which float on the top of the water are flat and cut into three half rounds. The leaves under water are cut into threads and spread out on all sides.

3. There is a great deal of duck-weed in our pond. Each plant has one little root in the water and a kind of stem at the top. It has no leaves. The tiny flowers sometimes come out of a slit in the side of the stem. Each flower is nothing but two dust-spikes and a tiny seed-box.

4. The bog-bean, or buck-bean, is nearly out of flower now. It grows at the edge of the pond, and its leaves are cut into three long parts. The pinkish flowers stand

WATER-MILFOIL

57

out on little stalks upon a tall stem. They are cup-shaped, with five points, and have a number of white hairs inside.

5. The water-milfoil grows almost all under water. Only the small pink flowers stand in a spike out in the air. The flowers at the top of the spike have only stamens in them. Lower down some have both dust-bags and seed-boxes. The ones at the bottom have seed-boxes, or ovaries, only. Milfoil leaves are narrow, like grass, but quite short. They stand round the stem like the spokes of a wheel, or the rays of a star.

BOGBEAN

Peggy's water-nosegay and show-card won the prize.

CPSIA information can be obtained
at www.ICGtesting.com
Printed in the USA
LVHW011324270723
753240LV00051B/144

Short Stories Series

by Shantia Kent

DORRANCE
PUBLISHING CO
EST. 1920
PITTSBURGH, PENNSYLVANIA 15238

The contents of this work, including, but not limited to, the accuracy of events, people, and places depicted; opinions expressed; permission to use previously published materials included; and any advice given or actions advocated are solely the responsibility of the author, who assumes all liability for said work and indemnifies the publisher against any claims stemming from publication of the work.

All Rights Reserved

Copyright © 2023 by Shantia Kent

No part of this book may be reproduced or transmitted, downloaded, distributed, reverse engineered, or stored in or introduced into any information storage and retrieval system, in any form or by any means, including photocopying and recording, whether electronic or mechanical, now known or hereinafter invented without permission in writing from the publisher.

Dorrance Publishing Co
585 Alpha Drive
Suite 103
Pittsburgh, PA 15238
Visit our website at www. dorrancebookstore. com

ISBN: 978-1-6393-7018-4
eISBN: 978-1-6393-7807-4

Happy very late Halloween
and late birthday Ms. T, Ms. Lou.
– your friend Shantia

One Shot's

My Sister Wallis. Horror

Theodora and Her Box of Good: Magical Realism and Drama

Auctioneer: Gothic /Drama & Mystery

Chapter 1

My Sister Wallis

Part 1

Years ago when I was thirteen-year-old, along with two of my friends, we were being yelled at by our older siblings, one of them was my older sister Wallis, for playing around the abandoned cottage house, then we all heard a very scowling male call out, "Get off my land!"

We ran like bats straight out of Hell out of that area! I was too terrified to ask anyone what happened on that day. Until years later, at age twenty-three, I got the courage to ask my sister Wallis, who was now thirty-one years old, about the history of about that abandoned cottage house. My sister Wallis sat me down and began telling me of about that cottage house.

Chapter 2

My Sister Wallis

Part 2

On that very land, a good-looking man built that cottage for his young bride for them to start a family together, but suddenly, after a half month, they disappeared without a trace. Years and years later after the couple disappeared, a farmer and his wife, along with their nine children lived in that cottage house. The farmer was not very friendly to his family; he was always drunk every day; he would always beat his family, until one day the farmer just snapped. He took an axe and killed his whole family.

The neighbors found out what the farmer did to his family; they all shot him to death.

Chapter 3

My Sister Wallis

Part 3

Years and years later, twin boys were found dead on that land of the cottage house; they were both hanged to death by a very heavy, very rusty chain around their necks. "Do you remember on that day me and your friends' older siblings were yelling at you guys for being there, Jen?"

"Yes," I said in almost quiet voice to Wallis. I replied, "Yes I do, Wallis."

"That very scowling male voice that scared us very badly on that day belonged to the murderous farmer, Jen." After Wallis finished that sentence, I was deeply terrified.

End

Chapter 1

Theodora and Her Box of Good: Persephone

An Inferno bride, no! I thought to myself. *If he thinks I am going to give up, then he is so wrong. I will get my Box of Good back from Damion, one way or another.* For a few months I acted like a good bride to Damion, earning his trust. He still made sure his servants kept a close eye on me.

The only time for me to begin my search for my Box of Good was in the dead of night when everyone was deeply asleep. I searched every inch of that cursed castle. But I couldn't find it anywhere, so I retreated back into my chamber quietly. I did cry myself to sleep on one of those nights, dreading on the countdown for my unholy wedding day that's coming very soon for me.

Chapter 2

Theodora and Her Box of Good:
New Name Is Pandora

Damion, the Entity of Evil, showed me around the Inferno Realm...
To those who have read, watched, or seen movies and paintings of
Hell, it was everything in one big package. The torment, screams of
agony and cries for help goes ignored. I can still hear it to this day.

Damion took me to his castle, where his servants stripped me
from my beautiful flowing ivory-white dress into a revealing black
velvet dress. They then braided my short, black, wavy hair with black
pearls in it. Then they put make-up on my face. When they were
done, Damion took a very good look at me and then said this: "Now
you look suitable as an Inferno bride, Theodora.

"Theodora...does not fit in your new life, so your new name will
be Pandora; it means "all gifted."

Chapter 3

Theodora and Her Box of Good: Entity of Evil

Hello, everyone. It's me, Theodora. Let's continue the story of my existence. I was tricked by a seeming innocent looking family who wanted help. I was fooled by them, the draw their magical hunting net and revealed themselves as infernal beings and dragged a twenty-four-year-old who wants to please her Creators and set the plan in motion for them.

But it didn't go as planned. The first lesson I learned was this: things can't go the way we want them to. When I got to the Supernatural Realm, I was kidnapped and was sold. That was the day I met the Entity of Evil. Also on that very same day, I never felt more fear than ever when he took me to the Inferno Realm.

Chapter 4

Theodora and Her Box of Good: Beginning

Everyone had parents, a childhood, and an upbringing in the beginning of their lives; for me, I didn't. I was created by the three Celestial Realm Rulers to be the Entity of Good. They give me beauty, clothing, wisdom, and skills. I was already a grown young adult, my age was twenty-four.

Then finally, the last two things they gave me was a name, Theodora Thomason, and my Box of Good. Then again, I was sent to the Supernatural Realm to release all the good there so it could spread there and then to the Human Realm.

Chapter 5

Theodora and Her Box of Good: Persephone

Damion's last words to me, before someone took me out of the Inferno Realm, were these: "Until we meet of again, Persephone." Then it all went black for me. When I woke up from my sleep, I was back in the Supernatural Realm in a field of flowers that had the blissful sun shining down on me with its warming ray. I let out of cry of joy to be there. I went to a stream to wash myself free, washing of away all my terrible experiences in the Inferno Realm. My short hair felt the small summer breeze go right through it while I used my power to change my black, tight, revealing dress into a no -revealing, flowing lavender dress along with matching long, soft sandals.

Then I went on to accomplish my mission that my Creators wanted me to do. I opened the Box of Good and let out the Seven Virtues: Humility, Kindness, Patience, Diligence, Charity, Temperance, and Chastity. They set out and spread their good virtues through the Supernatural Realm and the Human Realm.

Chapter 6

Theodora and Her Box of Good: Persephone

I had to keep telling myself to not fall into despair there, and I couldn't give and let that beast win, no matter what. So I waited for my chance. When it came, I took the opportunity. I never felt so happy to find my Box of Good, and now it was my time to escape the castle—and so I did—but getting out of there was not a very easy. I had to fight Damion servants. I fought very hard to get away from them.

When Damion found out that I got out, he was not very happy, and so we fought. In that fight we had, I didn't hold back. So I let loose all my power on him. The fight ended when someone took me of away from the Inferno Realm.

Chapter 7

Theodora and Her Box of Good: Persephone

After I finished my mission, I was sent back to the Celestial Realm. I was welcomed back home by the Rulers, who I thought I was never going to see them again. They gave me praise and sympathy for everything. I told them I never blamed them for what happened to me; they didn't know the whole thing was going to happen to me. We all hugged and cried. They made sure I went to therapy for help, got all the love and support from them that I needed. And also, I have a great job as a book editor. I'm forever grateful for them for all they did for me.

Centuries have come and went by fast for me. I was happy to be alive. But I have been through good times and bad times, loved and lost from those centuries. But I never gave up my hope and happiness that one day I will have a wonderful husband and a child.

Chapter 8

Auctioneer

Back when I was still six years old, I first met the Auctioneer: he was a tall dark brown headed man with hazel eyes and has ivory skin. He dressed very well for a very wealthy man. The Auctioneer came from very old money. From what my adopted Mother (Dayna Payton) told me. From what I recall about him the Auctioneer was more then a good-looking man: he was quite intelligent. His wife; whom name I don't even recall either was lovely as a rose and well-read... but she was arrogant. The wife had mid-long strawberry blonde hair, light blue eyes and light golden skin woman. The wife always dressed in the most extravagant clothes and jewelry. She loved being in the spotlight... so being a socialite fits her very well. Her origins is a complete mystery. The wife is hosting one of her parties with the Auctioneer social events to come. The couple would hire my mom one of the city seamstresses to make their clothes. She takes me (Heaven Payton) with her, when Grandma was out with her friends – when the Auctioneer was nice and a bit playful with man – his wife pay much attention to me. Mom didn't like the wide; for her bratty demeanor and treatment of her along with the servants. Many people had said the wife only married the Auctioneer for his money and she was having an affair behind her husband back. Many people had said the Auctioneer did or didn't know about his wife affairs or maybe he did not want to believe his beloved wife could do this to him.

The Auctioneer was soon to find out – the rumors to be true. When two of his employees showed the Auctioneer photo's – of his wife with two men.

After that, the Auctioneer wife along with her lovers were gone. No one asks about the Auctioneer wife and her two lovers disappearness, everyone was glad she's gone along with her two questionable lovers. But someone did call Law enforcements to investigation about this disappearness: the Auctioneer wife best friend named Belle and both of her lovers families. An investigation happened as everyone was questioned, my mom and me (Heaven) also, including the Auctioneer.

Time and things got in order – and well the Auctioneer was the Prime Suspect and he was arrested. During the trial the Auctioneer was a borderline manic – so it became a insanity and crime of passion case. He was sent to the Mental hospital… the Auctioneer was let go by the professionals early… Belle and the Auctioneer wife lovers Mothers couldn't believe it. To make matters more worst for them: they don't have whereabout of their love ones remains.

So yea Mom does not want to do business with him: She's told me it was bad voodoo for business. And that's it, I never saw him again.

CPSIA information can be obtained
at www.ICGtesting.com
Printed in the USA
LVHW011324270723
753240LV00051B/145

9 781639 370184